W9-BXX-507

THE LIBRARY OF
MEDIEVAL TIMES

Medieval Knights and Chivalry

Don Nardo

ReferencePoint
Press®

San Diego, CA

BRO
25.04 3/15

About the Author

Historian Don Nardo is best known for his books for young people about the ancient and medieval worlds. These include volumes on the histories, cultures, mythologies, arts, and literatures of the ancient inhabitants of Mesopotamia, Egypt, Greece, and Rome. Among his books about medieval times are studies of castles, warfare, arts and architecture, literature, religious pilgrimages, the Inquisition, the onset of the Black Death, the Viking invasions, and the trials of Joan of Arc and Galileo. Nardo also composes and arranges orchestral music. He lives with his wife, Christine, in Massachusetts.

© 2015 ReferencePoint Press, Inc.
Printed in the United States

For more information, contact:
ReferencePoint Press, Inc.
PO Box 27779
San Diego, CA 92198
www. ReferencePointPress.com

LIBRARY OF CONGRESS CATALOGING-IN-PUBLICATION DATA

Nardo, Don, 1947-
  Medieval knights and chivalry / by Don Nardo.
    pages cm. -- (Library of medieval times)
  Includes bibliographical references and index.
  ISBN-13: 978-1-60152-636-6 (hardback)
  ISBN-10: 1-60152-636-9 (hardback)
  1. Knights and knighthood--Europe--History 2. Chivalry--Europe--History. I. Title.
  U800.N37 2014
  940.1088'355--dc23
                                                                    2013040136

CONTENTS

IMPORTANT EVENTS OF MEDIEVAL TIMES

800
In Rome, Pope Leo III crowns Charlemagne emperor; his Carolingian dynasty rules western Europe until 987.

1000
A century of invention in farming begins; devices such as the heavy plow increase agricultural productivity and help double Europe's population.

632
The Prophet Muhammad dies as Islam begins to expand both east and west of the Arabian Peninsula.

ca. 950
Europe's first medical school opens in Salerno, Italy.

1099
The First Crusade ends Muslim rule in Jerusalem until 1187, when the Muslims under Saladin recapture Jerusalem from the Crusaders.

400	600	800	1000	1200

476
Romulus Augustulus, the last Roman emperor in the West, is dethroned.

1066
William of Normandy defeats the last Anglo-Saxon king at the Battle of Hastings, establishing Norman rule in England.

1200
The rise of universities begins to promote a revival of learning throughout the West.

1130
Church authorities in France ban tournaments; the ban on these popular festivals, which provide knights with opportunities to gain prestige and financial reward, is later reversed.

1184
Church officials meeting in Verona, Italy, approve burning at the stake as a punishment for anyone found guilty of heresy.

4

1215
King John of England signs the Magna Carta, limiting the rights of the monarchy.

1346
Using the longbow, English archers overwhelm the French army at the Battle of Crécy during the Hundred Years' War.

1328
Charles IV dies, ending 341 years of successful rule by the Capetian kings who established modern France.

1316
The Italian physician Mondino De' Luzzi writes the first book of the medieval period devoted entirely to anatomy.

1378
The Great Schism, in which there are three claimants to the papacy, occurs.

| 1250 | 1300 | 1350 | 1400 | 1450 |

1347
The deadly bubonic plague strikes Europe and returns intermittently for the next 250 years.

1337
The Hundred Years' War begins between France and England.

1453
The Ottoman Turks conquer Constantinople following a seven-week bombardment with cannons.

1267
Henry III of England enacts the Assize of Bread and Ale, one of the first laws to regulate the production and sale of food; the law ties the price of bread to the price of wheat, thus preventing bakers from setting artificially high prices.

1231
Pope Gregory IX establishes the "Holy Inquisition," whose purpose is to search out heretics and force them to renounce their views.

5

An Ongoing Fascination for Knights

Twenty-year-old Englishman William Marshal (1147–1219) beamed with pride and joy. On the eve of a battle in which he might well lose his life, his commander had bestowed on him an honor few individuals in Europe were destined to enjoy. In a solemn ceremony held in the Norman town of Drincourt in northern France, Marshal became a knight, a soldier of uncommon fighting skills, valor, and honor. In the part of the ceremony that took place in church, a priest handed him a sword and told him he was expected to use it for more than fighting the enemy. He must also employ the weapon to protect the poor and vulnerable from the rich and powerful. This was one of the rules of ethical behavior that made up the code of chivalry, or gallantry, that knights were supposed to follow.

The Ideal Knight

To Marshal's regret, much of the rest of the ceremony had to be cut short because the enemy the priest had mentioned was approaching fast. The year was 1164, and as happened quite often in the medieval era, the English and French were at war. During this conflict, a French army marched on Drincourt, and because the Normans and English were allies, a combined force of English and Norman soldiers hurried to defend the town. Among them was the newly knighted Marshal.

Once the opposing forces met, the fighting was fierce. During his first charge on horseback, William's lance broke, and seconds later his horse was badly wounded, forcing him to dismount and fight on foot. He saw French soldiers streaming into the town and followed as fast as he could. Catching up with them, the young knight hurled himself into their ranks and began swinging his sword with astounding speed, force, and accuracy. No other English or Norman troops had yet caught up, so for a few moments he fought the foe alone in the narrow, winding streets. Meanwhile, from windows above, droves of townspeople cheered him on and called for the Norman and English knights to come to his aid. "Up went the unanimous cry!" wrote Marshal's thirteenth-century biographer, who called himself John the Troubadour. "Over here all of you, to the brave knight's side! This man doesn't hide away, he makes great companies buckle before him, he cuts a swathe [path] through the ranks! He is a man whose blows strike home everywhere, a man who doesn't hold back, before whom lance and sword offer short resistance!"[1]

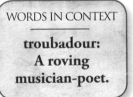

WORDS IN CONTEXT

**troubadour:
A roving
musician-poet.**

Eventually, Marshal's fellow knights came to his aid, and together they expelled the French from Drincourt. The incident marked the start of what became the most renowned career of any medieval European knight. According to multiple sources from the period, Marshal surpassed all the other knights in military prowess, honor, and loyalty to his colleagues and the four English kings he served (Henry II, Richard I, John, and Henry III). Marshal became known not only as an exceptionally fine fighter, but also as the perfect practitioner of medieval chivalry—in short, the ideal knight.

Varied Backgrounds and Personalities

Whether or not Marshal actually was the greatest medieval fighter and most honorable of all knights will likely never be known. Some knights built up sterling reputations that were considerably exaggerated over time. At the least, it is probably safe to say that Marshal and a handful of others like him were better fighters and more honorable men than many other knights.

After all, from the twelfth century on, thousands of knights existed in Europe in each new generation. They came from all sorts of backgrounds and possessed a wide array of different temperaments and personalities. It stands to reason that not all of them could be as heroic and chivalrous as Marshal, and in fact numerous writings from the period attest to the existence of knights who lied, cheated, raped, and murdered. Such knights were widely known and feared for their villainy as much as men like Marshal were renowned and revered for their decency.

Few, if any, European knights were cut from the idyllic cloth portrayed in the medieval romances—colorful tales of heroes and supremely noble characters like King Arthur and his knights Sir Lancelot and Sir Galahad. Real knights came in all sizes, abilities, and levels of honesty and honor. Modern historians have studied the surviving descriptions of those famous fighters and devised various general definitions for a knight of that era. In the words of one of the leading authorities on knights, Robert Jones, they consisted of "a group of men who formed a social elite as a result of their ability to fight from horseback in full armor, sharing a common set of values: chivalry."[2]

A More Perfect World?

Whatever these men were like in real life, their fame and society's fascination for them were not confined to the medieval centuries. Well after the knightly class declined in importance and influence in the sixteenth century, the image of the medieval knight lived on. Indeed, modern Western society retains a strong interest in old-style European knights and a special attraction to the model, highly chivalrous knight portrayed in the romantic literature. Among the images that have become iconic—symbolic or representative—of Europe's knightly period are mounted fighters covered from head to foot in metal armor; jousts—mock fights in which armored knights wielding long lances charged at each other; stone castles with moats and drawbridges,

WORDS IN CONTEXT

iconic: Symbolic or representative of something.

Medieval Europe, Circa 1250

where some knights lived; heroic quests in which knights searched for sacred objects for the glory of God; and romantic love affairs in which handsome knights courted beautiful maidens.

This ongoing contemporary fascination for European knights is reflected in the enormous number of popular nonfiction books, novels, movies, television shows, and video games featuring these special and in many ways unique warriors of a bygone age. "There can be no warrior quite so iconic and immediately recognizable as the medieval knight," Jones writes.

> More than any other, he remains a part of contemporary culture. Not only does he ride his charger, resplendent in his shining

armor and colorful heraldry through novels and movies, but his armor still decorates museums, castles, and stately homes, and his image in brass or stone adorns our churches. Every summer crowds gather to watch the sight of costumed interpreters bring him back to life in jousting matches and re-enactments.[3]

Various explanations have been suggested for why the image of the heroic medieval knight has come to be so deeply imbedded in the very fabric of Western civilization. Perhaps the most believable is that people in all times and places sometimes secretly wish they lived in a more perfect world. There the strong would not prey on the weak, because the latter would be protected by ever-present champions of goodness and law and order.

It is the kind of world described in a passage from a classic medieval romance telling about the origins of the noble Sir Lancelot. When humankind first appeared, the passage begins, "no man was higher in birth than any other." But over time, "envy and covetousness came into the world and might triumphed over right." So it became necessary to appoint certain men as guardians and defenders of the weak and humble. "They were the tall and the strong and the fair and the nimble and the loyal and the valiant and the bold."[4] Those special men were the knights.

WORDS IN CONTEXT

covetousness:
Greed.

CHAPTER ONE

The Rise of the Medieval Knight

The first literary depictions of European knights were penned by medieval writers, many of them Christian clergymen. The term *medieval* derives from the Latin phrase *medium aevum*, meaning "the age in the middle"—hence the other common name for the period, the Middle Ages. Historians view it as the period that separated ancient times from modern times and date it from roughly 500 to 1500 CE.

The vast majority of those medieval authors mistakenly believed that there had always been knights like the ones they saw around them. Scholars of that era knew a bit about ancient Greece and Rome, together constituting so-called Classical civilization, which had disappeared with Rome's fall in the fifth and sixth centuries. In the eyes of those scholars, the famous Roman military general Julius Caesar had been a knight. So had the renowned Macedonian Greek conqueror Alexander the Great. Moreover, it was common for leaders of the medieval kingdoms to claim that their peoples had descended directly from the "knights" who had fought in the Trojan War. In this view, Achilles, Hector, Odysseus, and the other heroes of that famous ancient conflict in which the Greeks had besieged Troy (in what is now Turkey) had all been armored knights much like those of medieval Europe.

Barbarians in the Ranks

Although this image of medieval-style knights inhabiting ancient Greece, Rome, and Troy turned out to be fanciful, it carried within it a grain of truth. In Greece, Rome, and a number of other well-developed preindustrial societies, the best and most respected warriors tended also to be members of the elite political and social classes. In both ancient and medieval Europe, in fact, usually only members of the wealthy classes could afford the finest armor, weapons, and horses. Of these items, horses and cavalry (mounted fighters) were often key. As Robert Jones points out:

> The development of mounted combat, using chariots at first, then horseback cavalry, was another way of reinforcing the status and superiority of the warrior and of the elite within the dominant class. The mount and its attendant equipment were expensive to obtain and maintain, and it took time to master the necessary riding skills to take a chariot or horse into battle, time and resources that only the elite could afford.[5]

Thus, the special medieval fighters called knights were not completely new in concept. Rather, they were the end product of a complex and long evolution that began in ancient Europe, especially during the Roman Empire's final centuries (around 300–500 CE). As Rome steadily declined in those years, so-called barbarian groups—mostly Germanic tribes from eastern and northern Europe—increasingly pressed on the realm's northern borders. Partly to pacify these tribes, Rome's government recruited some of their warriors into the Roman army's ranks. It seemed like a good idea at first. The Germans were good fighters, and when they served in the army, fewer native Romans had to become soldiers and risk their lives.

Over time, however, the policy proved counterproductive, at least to Rome. The percentage of barbarians in Roman armies kept increasing, while the preference of these warriors to fight independently rather than obey a chain of command caused serious discipline problems. Noted historian Arther Ferrill explains that the German recruits demanded

> great rewards for their service and showed an independence that in drill, discipline and organization meant catastrophe. They fought under their own native commanders, and the barbaric

system of discipline was in no way as severe as the Roman. Eventually, Roman soldiers saw no reason to do what barbarian troops in Roman service were rewarded heavily for not doing.[6]

The result was that fewer and fewer native Romans joined the military, which caused the government to step up recruitment of Germans even more. Finally, by about the year 440, the army of western Rome (the sector of the Empire centered in Italy) had become, in Ferrill's words, "little more than a barbarian army itself."[7]

Rise of the Medieval Aristocracy

For Rome, this trend proved tragic, since it helped to hasten the Empire's fall a few decades later from a combination of military, economic, and

Medieval scholars mistakenly believed that knights existed in earlier civilizations. They viewed the Macedonian Greek conqueror Alexander the Great (depicted entering Babylon) as a knight of great renown.

Adoption of the Stirrup

Early medieval mounted fighters did not enjoy the benefits of the stirrup. Most modern scholars believe that crucial military innovation was invented somewhere in China in the late first millennium BCE. It not only made mounting a horse less difficult than leaping onto it, but also allowed a rider to sit more securely and well balanced on the horse's back. The use of stirrups made its way from China to nearby India by the first century CE, and three centuries after that it was known in some sections of eastern Europe. There, the Huns, Avars, and other tribal peoples of the plains became some of history's greatest horsemen as a result of adopting the stirrup. Finally, the device appeared in western Europe at some point in the eighth or ninth century. Frankish cavalrymen in particular benefited, finding that they could remain seated on their steeds even when taking both hands off the reins to deploy their weapons. Moreover, a rider was able to briefly increase his height over an enemy horseman by standing in his stirrups. Stirrups alone did not make shock charges by cavalry highly effective. That happened only later, when horsemen adopted special saddles and lances in addition to stirrups.

other factors. But for the Germanic tribes and other northern European peoples who took over the remains of Rome's extensive provinces, the military training and experience many of their men had gained from Rome was a major boon. Despite what historians often call the "barbarization" of the late Roman army, that military machine had still been by far the finest in all Europe. So the Germans and other non-Romans in its ranks had been very effectively trained in the use of weapons and battlefield tactics.

That generation of post–Roman European soldiers became key to the continuing evolution of the medieval knight. After western Rome's government collapsed in the late 400s (while the Empire's eastern sector survived to become the Byzantine Empire), several small barbarian kingdoms formed across Europe. They were, in effect, the first medieval domains. In most cases, during the initial years of those fledgling realms, their chief warriors were the same men who had served successfully in the barbarian ranks of the Roman army.

For countless centuries in Europe, a nation's or society's leading warriors were also members of its social and political elites. Now, with Rome gone, this proved no different in Europe's early medieval kingdoms. The men who commanded the earliest post–Roman armies of these realms in the late 400s and early 500s saw that they could use the high military status they had earned as warriors to gain high social status as well. To this end, these local strongmen coalesced, or came together, into powerful landholding classes in their respective kingdoms.

Typically, a wealthy, respected former military commander became a powerful local lord with a following of loyal fighters of his own. He also controlled a number of peasant farmers. They either farmed his land or grew crops on lands he had given them and in return thereafter regularly supplied him with food. This system, which required a few generations to take hold on a large scale, gave rise to the landholding system of medieval Europe's aristocracy.

Masters and Apprentices

Meanwhile, the military establishments within the post–Roman European kingdoms developed to fit the needs of those societies. The sons, grandsons, and great-grandsons of their original military leaders in the late 400s and early 500s became leading warrior-aristocrats, too. "Well armed and well born," the late American historian C. Warren Hollister wrote, they "dominated their localities, providing the daily reality of military might translated into practical power."[8]

An essential part of that military might consisted of core groups of well-trained fighters that the kings and nobles could count on both to protect them and to fight for their interests. Some of the nobles themselves may have been, in a sense, very early versions of knights. But they were too few in number to form an early forerunner of the knightly class, and it was the fighters in those core groups that made up that early social group.

The origin of these special fighters was rooted in the reality that both late Roman generals and early medieval kings required companies of strong warriors to act as their bodyguards. In the 500s and 600s, these guards developed into two groups of elite warriors. One, called a *scara*, was a small but powerful unit of hardened, experienced soldiers who were completely loyal to their king or local lord. "This *scara* elite," military historian David Nicolle says, "seems to have fought as close-packed armored cavalry."[9]

The other elite group's members, known as *pueri*, were young men who apprenticed with the men of the *scarae*. After learning about weapons use and battle tactics from the finest existing military experts, the *pueri* became aristocratic elite warriors in their own right. Some experts think this bond between a master warrior and his trainee may have been an early version of what would later develop into the relationship between a medieval knight and the squire who trained under and aided him.

Enter the Franks

Most of the surviving evidence for these and other military developments in the early post–Roman European kingdoms comes from what is now France. In its earliest stages, the bulk of that region was called Francia, after the name of the people who settled there in large numbers in the 300s CE. The Franks, whom the Romans called Franci, were at first a loose alliance of Germanic tribes who pushed for and won slices of territory from the Roman government. Following the western Empire's collapse in the late 400s, the Frankish tribes became united under a dynasty of kings called the Merovingians.

The Merovingians ruled the Frankish kingdom until the 750s, when another family of rulers, the Carolingians, came to power. Their most successful and famous king was Charlemagne, who ruled from 768 to 814. A vigorous military leader, in the space of only a few years he created an empire that included not only all of France, but also large sections of what are now Germany, Italy, and Belgium. In the year 800 the reigning pope, Leo III, crowned Charlemagne emperor of what numerous people at the time viewed as a new Roman Empire. That new realm swiftly fell apart, however, after Charlemagne's death in 814.

The years encompassing these early lines of Frankish rulers, and especially Charlemagne's reign and the decades immediately following it, made up a defining period in the rise of the medieval knight, a cavalryman of uncommon skill. It was during this early portion of the medieval era that many of the key ideas and customs later associated with full-fledged knights developed. One of the most important was the use of cavalry and the tools and weapons of the mounted warrior.

Charlemagne, accompanied by troops on horseback, mounts an attack in Spain in 778. Ideas and customs associated with knights, such as the use of horses in warfare and weapons designed for mounted troops, developed around this time.

The fact that the first major use of cavalry in post–Roman Europe occurred in the Frankish kingdom was no accident. Other early European peoples bred and used horses but not to the degree the Franks did. One reason for this was that, years before, numerous rich Romans had established large horse-breeding estates in Francia, which was then known as Gaul. A hefty proportion of the horses Rome employed in warfare came from these rural domains. Later, after the Roman realm's demise, the early Franks inherited these estates and both dutifully and wisely maintained them.

Another important reason for Frankish supremacy in the early development of European cavalry was the nature of the Franks' enemies. Most of the major threats they faced came from peoples whose armies featured large units of mounted fighters. One example was the Avars, seminomadic tribesmen who originated in central Asia and threatened Europe in the 600s and 700s. Another Frankish enemy who employed cavalry consisted of Arab Muslims who invaded and conquered most of Spain in the early 700s. The Franks rightly reasoned that to counter these threats they had to develop their own large units of cavalry.

Armor and Weapons of the Era

The armor, weapons, and tactics employed by mounted Frankish soldiers were part of a formative stage of the classic European knights who developed later. The manner in which Frankish cavalrymen protected their upper bodies is a clear example. Like other early medieval horsemen of their era, they wore a chest protector called a *byrnie*, which was the single most expensive piece of armament they owned.

WORDS IN CONTEXT

byrnie: An early medieval chest protector made of leather covered by metal rings or scales.

The nature of the protective material that covered this somewhat bulky leather jerkin, or jacket, varied from place to place and maybe even from soldier to soldier. In some cases it was mail (sometimes called chain mail), consisting of attached rows of small iron rings. Other *byrnies* featured a mesh of little iron scales that had been sewn on using animal tendon or some other tough thread. Mail and scale armor provided a

18

An Early Model for the Knight

Full-fledged knights and the code of chivalry they adopted had not yet appeared in Charlemagne's day. Yet he was
such a feared and revered figure that in the years following
his death various medieval writers compiled popular tales,
often exaggerated or fictional, of his heroism and wisdom.
For Europeans in later centuries, therefore, Charlemagne
became an early model for the brave and chivalrous knight.
One of the earliest writings that projected this image was by
a ninth-century monk named Eginhard. In it Charlemagne
besieges a city, and instead of attacking it he wins over its
people through a great display of piety. At first, the residents
refuse to surrender. But then,

> the most inventive emperor said to his men: "Let us
> build today some memorial, so that we may not be
> charged with passing the day in idleness. Let us make
> haste to build for ourselves a little house of prayer,
> where we may give due attention to the service of
> God, if they do not soon throw open the city to us."
> No sooner had he said it than his men flew off in
> every direction, collected lime and stones, wood and
> paint, and brought them to the skilled workmen who
> always accompanied him. And between the fourth
> hour of the day and the twelfth they built . . . such a
> cathedral, . . . [and in this way he] took and occupied
> the city, without the shedding of blood, and merely
> by the exercise of skill.

Quoted in A.J. Grant, ed. and trans., *Early Lives of Charlemagne by Eginhard the Monk of St.
Gall*. London: Chatto & Windus, 1926, pp. 147–48.

soldier a fair amount of flexibility, making it easier for him to twist his body as necessary while fighting. But this ease of movement came at the expense of comprehensive protection. Although such armor could deflect the glancing blow of a sword or arrow, it could not stop a forceful direct thrust or puncture.

The weapons wielded by Frankish cavalrymen included spears, a short sword called a *seax*, and less often the bow. Most often a Frank hurled his spear overhand, hoping to strike the chest or face of an opponent. But he could also employ it underhand—for instance, when jabbing at the backs of fleeing enemy infantry, or foot soldiers. Frankish cavalry also sometimes used small round or oval-shaped shields. Exactly how often remains unclear, but there is no doubt that defending oneself with such a shield while holding the horse's reins and manipulating a spear or sword was extremely difficult and required a lot of skill and experience. Meanwhile, to protect his head, a horseman wore a thick leather cap or, if he could afford it, a metal helmet.

A fully armored Frankish cavalryman was likely a formidable sight. A contemporary monk's description of the great Charlemagne himself (also called Charles) decked out in his warrior's array has survived. "As the emperor drew nearer," it begins, one could see

> Charles, helmeted with an iron helmet, his hands clad in iron gauntlets [gloves], his iron breast and broad shoulders protected with an iron breastplate. An iron spear was raised on high in his left hand. His right always rested on his unconquered iron *falchion* [sword]. The thighs, which with most men are uncovered that they may the more easily ride on horseback, were in his case clad with plates of iron.[10]

This impressive collection of metal defensive and offensive gear was not at all typical of the average Frankish soldier, either mounted or on foot. Instead, it was peculiar to the only people who could afford it—the king and perhaps a handful of wealthy nobles. The average cavalryman could afford perhaps a mail jacket and a weapon or two, while many foot soldiers made do with a plain leather *byrnie* and a single weapon.

Frankish Cavalry Tactics

As was true of the armor and weapons of the Frankish cavalry, their bat-tlefield tactics were less developed than those of the full-fledged knights to come. Modern movies often depict early medieval horsemen taking part in shock action, or direct charges of cavalry units against either in-fantry or other horsemen. As Nicolle points out, however, in that era "real shock-cavalry charges were probably very rare."[11] This was partly because large-scale battles involving thousands of fighters hap-pened very infrequently in medieval times, especially in the Merovingian and Carolingian periods.

Also, and more importantly, early Frankish cavalry did not employ the stirrup, an Asian invention that did not reach western Europe until the late Carolingian era. Stirrups make it possible for a rider to stay upright and balanced in the saddle even when horse and rider en-counter an opposing force or obstacle. Without stirrups, the impact of a frontal assault on an enemy formation is likely to cause a rider to fall off his mount. Stirrups also allow a rider to easily mount his horse from the side by placing one foot in a stirrup and swinging the opposite leg up and over the steed's back into the other stirrup. Having no stirrups, Frankish and other early European cavalry vaulted onto their horses from the rear or side, like Muslim Arab horsemen did in this period.

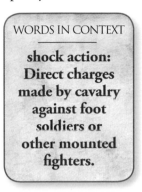

Even when stirrups appeared in western Europe in the eighth or ninth century, major shock action by cavalry remained rare, if it occurred at all, in battles fought by the Franks and their regular opponents. Most horse soldiers of the era acted as scouts, raided villages, and pursued fleeing enemies in the aftermath of a fight. On occasion they took more active and challenging roles on the battlefield. Nicolle explains that the several hundred cavalrymen making up a *scara* "were able to make coordinated flank [side] and rear attacks and to mount ambushes."[12]

Probably the most common tactic employed by these horsemen was to jump off their horses and fight like foot soldiers when commanded to do so by the war leader. In fact, "during the Middle Ages, most battles in the field saw most of the men who came to the battlefield on horseback dismount and fight on foot," scholar Bernard S. Bachrach points out.

Frankish cavalrymen protected their upper bodies by wearing bulky leather jerkins, similar to this one from around 1560. This item was the single most expensive piece of armament a horseback-riding soldier owned.

"Carolingian horsemen were trained to do this." Even the Normans, who arose in northwestern France and gained a reputation as tremendously accomplished horsemen, "far more often than not dismounted in battle in order to fight on foot,"[13] he says.

The main reason for this frequently used tactic was that, as has been shown, cavalrymen still had only limited value in battle if they were actually mounted. Put simply, the fastest way to get the army's best-armed and most experienced soldiers to the battlefield was to put them on horses. Once they reached the site of a fight, they were more effective as foot soldiers than as mounted ones.

This approach to using cavalry would soon change in dramatic fashion, however. The full-blown medieval knight was about to emerge. A highly specialized fighter, he was destined to transform warfare, and society too, in ways that even the great military commander Charlemagne could not have foreseen.

CHAPTER TWO

The Height of Knights in War and Society

The evolution of early European cavalrymen into knights continued into the medieval era's second major phase—the so-called High Middle Ages. That period, in which full-fledged knights emerged and reached their height, is usually dated from the eleventh through the sixteenth centuries (around 1000 to 1500). The cavalrymen who made up elite units like the *scarae* in early medieval times "were set apart by their expensive equipment and horses,"[14] scholar Frances Gies explains. However, they had not yet emerged as a separate and broadly venerated division of European society in their own right. The knights of eleventh-century Europe and beyond, on the other hand, were members of a distinctive and widely respected social class. "Gradually," Gies continues,

> professional pride matured into class consciousness, which was enhanced by the church's sponsorship. The soldiers of the early medieval period may or may not properly be called knights, but the full development of knighthood came only with the acquisition of class identity. The western European knight may be summarized as a mounted, heavily armed and armored soldier, in most times and places a free man and a landholder, and, most significantly, a member of a class with a strong sense of solidarity.[15]

The Character of a Knight

The character of the men making up this special social group was shaped by four intertwined attributes. The most obvious was a knight's military prowess, the impressive fighting skills that took years to master. Another consisted of his social status, which usually made him either a nobleman or the close associate or follower of a nobleman.

The third facet of a knight's character was defined by economic factors. At the very least, he owned a horse and some decent armor and weapons, things that the average person could not afford. Beyond those significant belongings, some knights were virtually penniless. They relied on the loot they gained during military campaigns or else the support, including lodgings, they might receive from the nobleman they worked for. Other knights either started out with or over time gained considerable wealth, including money, land, and in some cases a castle.

Finally, the knight had a religious and moral dimension. It was based partly on his oath to serve God; most European knights were quick to defend the church and fight its enemies. There was also the fact that the knightly class adopted a code of ethical behavior—chivalry. Even though individual knights did not always behave in ethical ways, society expected a knight to at least try to do so.

WORDS IN CONTEXT

hauberk: Worn by knights during the High Middle Ages; a long protective jerkin or jacket covered with mail.

Expansion of Defensive Armor

The most visible of these major facets of knighthood—military prowess—developed directly out of the cavalry units employed by the Franks and a few other European peoples in the sixth through tenth centuries. That development is easiest to follow by examining the continued evolution of the mounted warrior's defensive armor. The protective gear used by cavalry in Charlemagne's time was more extensive than that of horse soldiers in prior centuries, and such ongoing multiplication of armor persisted in the centuries that followed.

By the early to mid-1000s, for example, *byrnies* had become considerably longer and heavier. The elongated version, which came to be called a *hauberk*, hung to the knees. To make it possible for the rider to spread his legs wide enough to mount his steed, makers of hauberks added a long slit in its bottom section.

Several other parts of the body also received increased protection in this period of the emerging knight. One such protection was the coif, a cloth or leather hood covered with mail, which enveloped the top, back, and sides of the head. Over time the coif developed an extra flap that could be pulled across a man's lower face. By the early 1100s knights also started wearing mail-covered arm and leg protectors and thick gloves with flared extensions in the back to protect the wrists. About a half century later, they also began to don the surcoat, a loose cloth outer garment that hung over the hauberk. The surcoat's initial purpose was to shade the mail on the *hauberk* from the sun so that the metal rings would not absorb too much heat and slowly bake the wearer.

The steady expansion of the knight's defensive equipment continued at a brisk pace, often because offensive weapons were becoming more lethal. By the year 1200 or so, for instance, it was common to wear a round or conical iron skull cap under the coif, which by itself was not sufficient to stop direct, savage blows by large swords. Similarly, in time the mail *hauberk* did not prove strong enough to deflect such blows, so knights asked armor makers to insert plates of sheet metal along the inner surfaces of both *hauberks* and surcoats.

This helped. But enemy fighters learned to aim their sword thrusts at the weakest spots—the joints where the plates abutted one another. To protect against such thrusts, in about 1250 armored suits began featuring cup-shaped metal pieces that fit over the knees, elbows, and other joints. At the same time, many knights deemed it necessary to clothe their horses in armor similar to their own. That way, it was harder for an opponent to put a knight at a disadvantage by wounding or killing his mount.

Eventually, military historian Archer Jones writes, "a complete suit of plate armor, which protected the wearer from the shock of blows and deflected both hand weapons and crossbow bolts, became

A fully armored horse and rider, like this one from the fifteenth century, had an advantage over an enemy who lacked such protection. But heavy armor worn by both horse and rider could also slow a soldier down in battle.

common." This new reality had both strengths and drawbacks, Jones points out:

> A suit of the new armor could weigh seventy pounds, and, together with its own armor, the horse had to carry over 100 pounds of metal alone. With a horse protected from lance wounds in the chest and the rider virtually proof against harm, the knight became far more formidable. However, this alteration both raised the cost of the mounted man and seriously reduced his mobility. The heavier burdened horse found it harder to gallop and the rider had difficulty in executing any maneuver but the straight-ahead charge.[16]

A Knight's Principal Weapons

The loss of mobility resulted partly from the sheer weight of the knight's defensive equipment. In addition, the pieces of armor that overlapped the knees and other joints caused a certain amount of reduction in his flexibility of movement. As a result, it was no longer practical to employ all the weapons that cavalrymen had in prior centuries. The bow was the first to go. Not long afterward, knights abandoned the spear, too.

By the late eleventh and early twelfth centuries, the knight's main weapon had become the broadsword. With a longer, wider blade than the versions used in the Carolingian era, it was designed mainly as a slashing device. But as European cavalry armor grew steadily heavier, many broadswords developed more pointed tips. This gave them a better chance of piercing metal plates. The most common sword used by European knights in the twelfth century and beyond, Robert Jones writes, had "broad, flat blades that tapered gently and terminated in a round point, and short, single-handed grips. In the 13th century, the longer 'great sword' or 'war sword' appeared, whose blade, while of the same cross-section as earlier forms, was made longer, as was the grip, which enabled it to be used with two hands."[17]

Advantages of the Couched Lance

A leading modern historian of medieval history and culture, Richard Barber, here discusses one of the key military developments that helped to make possible the emergence in Europe of a large class of heavily armored knights. "This," he says, "was the use of the couched lance by a group of horsemen who mounted a closely coordinated charge as a single unit." Before the introduction of the couched lance, Barber explains,

> there had been three alternative methods of wielding the lance, which was one of the main weapons of war. It could be used as a javelin to hurl overarm at the enemy, or it could be used as a spear to be held either overarm or underarm to jab at the opponent. The disadvantage to all three methods was that once the lance had made contact, it was difficult to retrieve it and therefore the warrior was left vulnerable. The couched lance, on the other hand, was held tightly tucked under the right arm so that a heavier (and more effective) lance could be used. The full weight of man and horse was behind each blow and the warrior was distanced from his opponent, making him less vulnerable to attack. Unless it broke in the onslaught, the lance was retained by the knight, who could use it repeatedly if required to do so.

Richard Barber and Juliet Barker, *Tournaments: Jousts, Chivalry, and Pageants in the Middle Ages.* Woodbridge, UK: Boydell and Brewer, 2000, p. 14.

A second principal weapon wielded by the heavily armored knight was the lance. Initially, it consisted of an uncomplicated, fairly light pole about 10 to 12 feet (3 to 3.7 m) long. Over time, however, it got thicker and heavier. It also came to feature a flared section in the back to protect the fighter's hand and lower arm.

The lance was clearly intended to strike an enemy horseman's upper body and knock him off his steed. But the weapon was effective only if the man using it was able to stay on his own mount when the tip crashed into his opponent. The stirrup gave the lance-wielding knight a certain amount of traction but was not foolproof by itself. It was necessary, in addition, to develop a bigger, much wider saddle with a large pommel. With such a saddle, the rider could rest the back, or butt, of the lance on the pommel, which absorbed a major portion of the shock of a strike.

This distinctive approach became known as the "couched lance" method. When it came into wide use beginning around 1100, it was possible for a line of knights to conduct a cavalry charge featuring a long row of level, projecting lances. It was a devastating tactic, especially when employed against infantry, who at the time had great difficulty countering it.

From Wartime to Peacetime

Thus, the heavily armored European knights who fought during the 1200s, 1300s, and 1400s were often highly lethal and successful in battle, giving them formidable reputations as fighters. Yet there was always the danger that they might lose some of their effectiveness due to over-confidence. Because they were elite warriors, and also because some of them belonged to the upper classes in their native realms, these men were often proud, vain, and arrogant. As a result, lack of discipline in their ranks was a recurring problem. According to researchers James F. Dunnigan and Albert A. Nofi:

> Foot soldiers were disdained [by most knights] and discipline was seen as incompatible with a noble warrior's honor. The basic problem was that every [knight] thought he was above obeying orders. A duke or a count had some control over his knights, but each such noble was less impressed by the royal official, or king himself, in charge of the entire army. Every noble thought he, and his troops, deserved the post of honor in the first rank [in a battle]. An army commander would try to line up his various contingents in such a way that each would be used to best effect. But most knights simply wanted to get at the enemy and fight it out man to man.[18]

Some modern scholars have argued that one reason knights were so eager to fight and prove themselves in battle is that they were easily bored by the routines of ordinary life. The late, renowned expert on medieval society Marc Bloch, for instance, pointed out that these men did not have normal jobs and suggested that they frequently became restless in peacetime. "Accustomed to danger," Bloch wrote, the knight often found that "everyday life easily slipped into a gray monotony."[19]

Other scholars counter that this may have been true for some knights but by no means all. According to this view, when not involved in mili-

Castles built from stone, with drawbridges and towering defensive walls, began to appear in Europe in the eleventh century. Wealthy knights or those who distinguished themselves in battle might be awarded land and a castle of their own.

Rituals of a Novice Knight

In his account of the dubbing of young Geoffrey of Anjou into knighthood in 1128, medieval chronicler Jean of Tours went into considerable detail about the traditional rituals Geoffrey enacted following his ceremonial bath. These included his acceptance of an array of beautifully made armor and weapons.

Geoffrey donned a linen undergarment, a tunic of gold cloth, a purple robe, silk stockings, and shoes ornamented with golden lions. His attendants, who were being initiated into knighthood with him, also put on gold and purple. With his train of nobles, Geoffrey left the chamber to appear in public. Horses and arms were brought and distributed. A Spanish horse of wonderful beauty was provided for Geoffrey, swifter than the flight of birds. He was then armed with a corselet of double-woven mail which no lance of javelin could pierce, and shod with iron boots of the same double mesh. Golden spurs were girded on [attached]. A shield with golden lions was hung around his neck. A helmet was placed on his head, gleaming with many precious stones, and which no sword could pierce or mar. A spear of the ash [tree] tipped with iron was provided, and finally, from the royal treasury was brought an ancient sword.

Quoted in Frances Geis and Joseph Gies, *Life in a Medieval Castle*. New York: HarperCollins Row, 1979, pp. 166–67.

tary campaigns, many knights had plenty of duties and personal pursuits to keep them busy and mentally stimulated. Typically, many of the less-well-off knights were retainers (or vassals). That is, in wartime they fought for the king or noble to whom they owed allegiance, but in peacetime they lived in and guarded that lord's castle.

Emergence of Stone Castles

Large stone castles like those often seen in movies about Robin Hood and King Arthur developed roughly in tandem with armored knights. Before the eleventh century, when the multiplication of knightly armor was in its early stages, the few castles that existed in Europe were usually little more than two- or three-story wooden structures surrounded by wooden stockade fences. They were almost always erected on a hilltop to make them more easily defendable. The key turning point was Norman king William the Conqueror's invasion and seizure of England in 1066. Only after that, thanks to the building programs he initiated, did true castles—made of stone and featuring drawbridges and towering defensive walls and battlements—begin to appear.

For rulers like William, as well as their chief nobles and knights, the castle became the central focus of life and activity on a typical manor, or country estate. Within the castle itself, the center of life was the "great hall," or more simply "the hall." A sort of combination of throne room, meeting place, and dining commons, it was where the king or lord conducted business and ate and conversed with his live-in retainers. Those knights slept either inside the main residence or in a nearby outbuilding. In addition to protecting the castle and manor, they performed various duties, including training would-be knights and other fighters for the monarch or lord.

In contrast, well-to-do knights earned or were awarded manors of their own, some complete with castles. Such estates featured cooks, butlers, and other servants in the residence; peasant farmers to work the land; and usually the knight-owner's own loyal retainers. Managing all of these people was a major undertaking, although some owners hired professional managers, called bailiffs, to do such work.

A Knight in Training

Whatever positions knights found themselves in during peacetime, they were not necessarily restricted to activities like protection, training for war, and managing their own estates. A number of knights also devoted considerable time to more aesthetic pursuits—those involving artistic or other personal talents. First and foremost, the vast majority of knights were literate during an age when most people could neither read nor write. As Gies puts it, "It was a poor knight who could not read and write."[20] Partly for this reason, a good many knights became poets, chroniclers, or diarists. England's famous William Marshal, for instance, was only one of the many knights who proudly composed poetry.

In most cases men of the knightly class learned to read and write when they were squires training to become knights. If a young man was not already literate when he became a squire, his king or lord assigned him a tutor. The latter not only taught him reading skills but also introduced him to certain areas of learning then seen as desirable for educated people. These included history, astronomy, and especially the Bible and various other Christian writings. A surviving medieval narrative tells how a tutor "attended his pupil everywhere, took him to school, prevented him from eating too much, taught him polite language and good manners, and did not even quit him when he dressed and when he retired to bed."[21] Indeed, squire and tutor worked together so closely and for so long that the older man became an extremely important and memorable figure in the younger one's life.

Meanwhile, the squire worked with his master, the knight he had been assigned to, as well as various trainers and weapons experts, on improving his physical conditioning and fighting skills. The young man learned how to ride a horse with great proficiency. He also became adept with a knight's traditional weapons—the sword, the lance, and to a lesser degree the mace (club). For practice, the squire attacked a *quintain*, a shield-covered dummy mounted on a tall post. There was also a great deal of swordplay and other sparring with the trainers and at times the master himself.

The length of a squire's apprenticeship differed from place to place and from one time period to another. But four to eight years was fairly typical. All during those years, the young man was expected to pay back the lord, knight, and trainers by performing various regular menial duties. Among the more common ones were feeding and grooming the horses, cleaning out the stables, polishing the master's armor, waiting on the master and other knights and/or nobles during mealtimes in the castle's great hall, and helping to clean up the kitchen afterward.

The Dubbing Ceremony

At the end of a squire's training period, he finally had the privilege of being dubbed, or appointed, a full-fledged knight. This could happen almost anytime and anywhere. However, evidence suggests that knightly dubbings most often occurred in three specific situations—during a major courtly ceremony, such as the coronation of a king or the wedding of a king or lord; during a pilgrimage to an important shrine, especially in the Holy Land; and on the eve of battle. The latter situation was exemplified by Marshal's dubbing in the moments before the French attacked Drincourt in 1164.

By the thirteenth century the dubbing ceremony had become quite complex and stately. Local nobles and other dignitaries attended, and clergymen blessed the knight and his weapons. There was a preliminary ritual bath for the candidate, and often he cut his hair short, in the style worn by monks, to demonstrate his reverence for God. At the height of the ceremony, the king or other presiding nobleman recited words that varied a bit from place to place but can be approximated as "Knight, God grant you a life of honor, that you may be a man of great trust and worth, in thought, word, and deed."[22] The formality and complexity of this ceremony, along with years of extensive training and the mastery of devastating weapons and battlefield tactics, became hallmarks of the knightly class, whose members were among the finest and most feared fighters Europe had ever seen.

CHAPTER THREE

Code of Chivalry: Ideal Versus Reality

Chivalry was made up of special rules of behavior that became closely associated with medieval European knights. The late historian Maurice Keen, one of the leading authorities on medieval chivalry, called it "the secular code of honor of a martially oriented aristocracy."[23] By *secular*, he meant that chivalry's regulations operated outside the control of the church. Thus, the warlike nobility he described, with its widely admired superstars, the knights, developed its own set of tenets, or guiding laws.

European knights' goal in adopting chivalry, one they almost never openly voiced, was to police themselves. The frightening perceived alternative was that the overwhelming physical power and brute force they possessed might run amok and reduce society to a state of barbarism. Robert Jones points out that chivalry was also "the criteria by which the knights measured themselves" as human beings. He adds, "Although principally militaristic, chivalry presented ideals of behavior both on and off the battlefield, and became an ideology that was to encompass all aspects of its adherents' lives."[24]

Origins of Chivalry

Modern historians date the so-called age of chivalry from about 1100 to the early 1500s. During the initial years of that period, the chivalric honor code developed out of three major areas of influence. The first was a strong warrior ethic inherited from the late Roman army, the barbarian tribes that overran Rome, and the Franks and other early Europeans whose kingdoms arose in the regions once occupied by the Romans and barbarians. This warrior ethic emphasized such qualities as bravery, skill in the use of weapons, and loyalty to one's comrades in arms. Over time these largely martial ideals became overlaid with others derived from romantic literature, such as fighting fair. That is, a good and decent knight was expected to suppress his natural urge to cheat and employ underhanded tactics to win a fight.

> **WORDS IN CONTEXT**
>
> **martial: Warlike, militaristic, or aggressive.**

A second area of influence that contributed to the rise and shape of chivalry was the high social position that most knights enjoyed. Personal virtue became partly associated with the powers of large landholders, for instance, a country lord's ability and duty to mete out justice to the social inferiors who worked for him. Such wealthy individuals were close to the king and his royal court. So the rules of chivalry were also influenced by courtly activities like poetry writing, music and dance, and gentlemanly men wooing and marrying women from polite society. In this regard, the fictional court of King Arthur became a model to emulate.

The third area of influence on chivalry's development consisted of religious idealism. Although the medieval church had little or no control over what knights did, they were devout men who wanted to please God. If God, as leading churchmen preached, was *against* violence for the sake of violence, the counterargument was that God must be *for* violence that had a noble purpose. In this way, the concept of fighting a "just war" on behalf of God became a tenet of the chivalric code. This was the reasoning that drew so many European knights so strongly to the cause of the Crusades. A series of wars lasting from 1095 to the late 1200s, their goal was to free the Holy Land, thought to have been established by God along the Mediterranean's eastern coast, from the Muslims who had seized control of it.

Various Chivalric Qualities

Europe's medieval code of chivalry included a number of attractive and/or charming qualities or values that made the knights who ascribed to them appear special in the eyes of most people. Part of what made knights so appealing and widely respected, for example, was that they took a solemn oath to a king or nobleman to defend him with their lives. This selfless act was seen as both courageous and chivalrous. Eloquence, or speaking well, was also viewed as chivalrous, as was displaying skills in hunting, courtly games, and other activities associated with wealthy folk and courtly life.

A surviving document from the 1100s, which describes a French knight of that period named Folcon, stresses these and some other qualities of chivalry. When his king caught sight of him in the military ranks before a battle, that ruler turned to some French officers and declared, "Look at the best knight you have ever seen!" The king then launched into an inventory of Folcon's chivalrous traits, saying,

> He is brave, and courtly, and skillful, and noble, and of good lineage, and eloquent, and handsomely experienced in hunting and falconry. He knows how to play chess, and backgammon, and gaming, and dicing. [And] he has never been slow to perform honorable deeds. He dearly loves God and the Trinity. And since the day he was born he has never entered a court of law where any wrong was done or discussed without his grieving if he could do nothing about it.[25]

A late thirteenth-century French romance, *Durmart le Galois*, echoed some of these same chivalric qualities and added a few more. "A knight must be hardy," it stated. He should also be "courteous; generous; loyal and fair of speech; ferocious to his foe; and frank and debonair [charming] to his friend."[26]

Love and Respect for God

Of all these chivalric qualities, among the more important was piety, as exemplified by the phrase "he dearly loves God" in the statement of praise for the knight Folcon. One of a knight's greatest possessions, of course, was his prowess, meaning his military skills. There was a sense

Departing knights bid farewell to their ladies. Personal virtue, and courtly activities such as poetry writing and the wooing of women from polite society, all helped to shape medieval chivalry.

among many knights, and definitely among numerous medieval writers, that such prowess was a gift from God to be treasured and used always for good. "Earning honor by prowess appears throughout most chivalric literature as complementary to the worship of God," University of Rochester historian Richard W. Kaeuper explains. "Approval for prowess—at least for prowess in the right causes—comes not only from humans, but descends from highest heaven. In fact, God opens wide the doors of paradise for his brave knights."[27]

This concept—that one of chivalry's most vital values was divine approval of knights' military talents—is well illustrated in a surviving document by a twelfth-century monk, Guibert of Nogent. A passage says that knights who went on crusade were doing God's work. Furthermore, God had actually *instigated* such holy wars in part so that Christian knights could be saved, or achieve heaven, while pursuing

Wicked and Evil Folk Fear Knights?

Some medieval churchmen defended the dark, violent side of knighthood and chivalry, arguing that violence and even bloodshed were sometimes necessary to protect the church and clergy against various forces that threatened them. This argument was voiced by the anonymous author (whom modern scholars suspect was a priest) of the *Ordene de Chevalerie, or Order of Knighthood*, penned in France around 1220. (The use of the word *us* in the passage refers to clergymen, to whom the work was addressed.)

Knights, whom everybody should honor, are created [by God], for they have us all to guard. And if it were not for knighthood, our lordship [authority] would be of little worth, for they defend Holy Church, and they uphold justice for us against those who would do us harm. I will not refrain from praising knights. He who does not love them is very foolish. Our chalices [holy cups] would be stolen from before us at the table of God, and nothing would ever stop it. But their justice, which defends us in their persons, is decisive. The good would never be able to endure if the wicked did not fear knights, and if there were only Saracens, Albigensians, and Barbarians, and other people of evil faith who would do us wrong. But these [wicked folk] fear knights, and one should hold knights more dear and glorify and honor them!

Quoted in Raoul de Hodenc, Keith Busby, ed. and trans., *Le Roman des Eles* and Anonymous, *Ordene de Chevalerie*. Amsterdam: John Benjamins, 1983, pp. 174–75.

their obviously violent occupation. Guibert claimed, "God in our time has introduced the holy war so that the knighthood and the unstable people, who shed each other's blood in the way of pagans, might have a new way to win salvation. They need not choose the life of a monk and abandon the world in accordance with the vows of a rule [meaning a monastery], but can obtain God's grace through their own profession."[28]

Guibert's more famous contemporary, churchman and writer Bernard of Clairvaux, agreed. Bernard went even further by suggesting that crusading knights were ministers as well as warriors of God. This, he said, was because, like clergymen, they fought against evil and evildoers. "The knight of Christ, I say, may strike with confidence and die yet more confidently, for he serves Christ when he strikes, and serves himself when he falls. Neither does he bear the sword in vain, for he is God's minister, for the punishment of evildoers and for the praise of the good. If he kills an evildoer, he is not a mankiller, but, if I may so put it, a killer of evil."[29]

Together, these and other positive qualities described in the medieval romances and chronicles were what most Europeans of that era viewed as hallmarks of chivalry. Because knights were routinely associated with these values, minstrels frequently idolized these elite fighters in popular songs and poems. One minstrel sang that it gave him "great joy to see" knights lined up in their colorful battle array. "And my heart is filled with gladness when I see strong castles besieged [by such knights, and] when the battle is joined, let all men of good lineage think of nothing else but the breaking of heads and arms. For it is better to die than be vanquished and live."[30]

Rampages and Pillage

Whatever they promised in their oaths when they were dubbed, many knights did not always uphold these widely accepted values of chivalry. Some knights who started out with every intention of doing so lost their way over time. They gave in to the temptation to use their social position, formidable military abilities, and wealth if they had it to bully and intimidate people. Some others never intended to follow the rules of chivalry in the first place. For them, the pursuit of knighthood was merely a means to an end, a convenient way to acquire the stature, affluence, and reputation needed to be powerful, influential, and feared.

WORDS IN CONTEXT

affluence:
Wealth or a very
comfortable
lifestyle.

Whatever their initial motivations may have been, it became common for some knights to take full advantage of their power by brutalizing ordinary people and pillaging houses and entire towns. This sort of reprehensible behavior was almost routine during wartime. In 1217, for instance, an army led by William Marshal and other knights loyal to King Henry III attacked the rebellious city of Lincoln (in east-central England). In the battle's aftermath, the knights ordered and took part in a horrendous display of robbery, pillage, and general destruction, captured in English chronicler Roger of Wendover's *Flowers of History*. The knights, he wrote,

> plundered the whole city to the last farthing, [and] next pillaged the churches throughout the city and broke open the chests and storerooms with axes and hammers, seizing on gold and silver in them, clothes of all colors, women's ornaments, gold rings, goblets and jewels. Nor did the cathedral church escape this destruction, but underwent the same punishment as the rest. . . . When they had thus seized on every kind of property, so that nothing remained in any corner of the houses, they each returned to their lords as rich men.[31]

Indeed, engaging in such out-and-out theft was on the whole a major source of the wealth accumulated by many of the more successful, well-to-do knights. Moreover, sometimes such rampages were not motivated simply by greed for loot. They were also driven by a naked bloodlust—a manic, almost uncontrollable urge to kill—that has periodically affected at least some of the soldiers in armies throughout history, including the present century.

A number of upper-class medieval writers even glorified such behavior. One of their number was the twelfth-century French poet Bertrand de Born. He viewed the brutal abuse of townspeople and peasants by knights, as well as the battlefield deaths of the knights themselves, as a sort of quaint pageantry. In one of his narratives, he proclaimed that he was delighted to watch knights "scatter people and herds in their path." Also, "I tell you, I find no such savor in food, or in wine, or in sleep, as in hearing the shout, 'On! On!' from both

Knights wage a fierce battle at the walls of a castle. After achieving their hard-fought victory, the knights often entered the castle or town to rob, rape, and pillage.

sides, and the neighing of steeds that have lost their riders, and the cries of 'Help! Help!' in seeing men great and small go down [in agony] on the grass beyond the castle moat; in seeing at last the dead, the decorated stumps of lances still in their sides."[32]

The Threat of Violence

In fact, abundant evidence shows that in spite of the benefits to society when knights honorably strove to enforce the code of chivalry, the threat of unlawful, decidedly unchivalrous violence always lurked. All through the High Middle Ages, average citizens of the European kingdoms were forced to recognize a regrettable fact of life. Namely, they had as much reason to fear knights as they did to admire them. In his landmark study of medieval knights, Kaeuper states that in that era Europeans

> increasingly found the proud, heedless violence of knights, their praise for settling any dispute by force, and for acquiring any desired goal by force on any scale attainable, an intolerable fact of social life. Such violence and disorder were not easily compatible with other facets of the civilization they were forming. We will misunderstand chivalry if we fail to set it squarely in the context of this knightly violence.[33]

There were, therefore, two contradictory facets or dimensions of medieval knightly chivalry. One was bound up in the brightly wrapped and decorated package of the ideal qualities of knighthood. These were the positive values that knights like Marshal actually practiced. It has been established, however, that even the most honorable knights, Marshal included, condoned horrific displays of violence and injustice in certain specific situations. His participation in the shameful pillage of the town of Lincoln in 1217 is a clear example.

Another example of a situation in which bloody violence by knights was acceptable was the killing of one knight by another. As long as it was seen to be a fair fight, such butchery was actually something to be admired, even marveled at. That martial concept, equating the slaughter of other men as virtuous, absolutely riddles the chivalric romances, including the extensive Arthurian legends and poems.

One of the more popular tales of King Arthur's chief knight, Lancelot, refers to "the great marvels of his prowess, which had been testified

In his groundbreaking and widely influential book, *Chivalry and Violence in Medieval Europe,* scholar Richard W. Kaeuper argues that chivalry had a dark side. He presents abundant literary and other evidence showing that medieval nobles, churchmen, and writers consistently praised the violent, destructive side of knighthood, accepting it and knights' use of force to get their way as a fact of life.

We must recognize how strongly chivalric literature acknowledges the impulse to settle any issue—especially any perceived affront to honor—by couching the lance for the charge or swiftly drawing the sword from the scabbard. Force is regularly presented as the means of getting whatever is wanted, of settling whatever is at issue. Accusations of a more or less judicial [sensible] nature, [quite often] lead to a fight, as does assertion of better lineage [ancestry]. But so does assertion that one's lady is fairer than another knight's lady, a request for a knight's name, or even an answer to the question, "Why are you so sad?" Of course, as often as not, the fight is over no stated question at all, but simply seems a part of the natural order of the imagined world of chivalry. Two knights meet in the forest, and they fight. [Filled with such primitive aggression] the vast and complex literature of chivalry celebrates knightly violence.

Richard W. Kaeuper, *Chivalry and Violence in Medieval Europe.* New York: Oxford University Press, 2001, pp. 159–60.

to in many places, and shown to be true, for he split knights and horses and heads and arms and lances and shields, and beat down knights to the right and left." Other soldiers involved in a battle with him were so impressed that they stopped fighting long enough to watch Lancelot "and see the marvels he performed."[34]

A Terrible Reality

Many European knights took such passages seriously enough to model themselves on literary characters like Lancelot. As a result of such attitudes, similar violence sometimes crossed over into real life and was duly admired by most of the writers who witnessed it. In 1381 a French knight named Robert Salle clashed with a group of English knights, an event recorded by the famous French chronicler Jean Froissart. Robert "drew a long Bordeaux sword," Froissart wrote, "and began cutting and thrusting all around him, a lovely sight to see. Few dared to come near him, and those who did, he cut off a foot or a head or an arm or a leg with every stroke he made."[35]

Moreover, such displays were condoned by other members of the upper classes, of which knights were charter members. Even kings supported the use of licit, or legal and acceptable, violence when they felt it

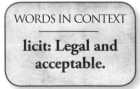

was in their own best interests. In fact, Kaeuper argues, numerous medieval kings actually attempted to create "a royal monopoly over licit violence."[36] That is, these monarchs realized that in order for them to hold on to power, it was sometimes necessary to resort to naked aggression, even when unprovoked. Furthermore, Kaeuper says, "their work as kings was complicated by two significant facts: Kings, too, were knights and generally believed in a code that enshrined violence; and they needed the knights as part of their administrations and as a key element in their military force."[37]

Many kings and their loyal knights who were well meaning, like Marshal, preferred it if they could get something they wanted without using bully tactics or open aggression. But almost none of them were completely above such behavior. Meanwhile, less honorable knights, who may well have significantly outnumbered men like Marshal, were more likely to unleash such violent outbursts more unpredictably.

This created a constant tension, a level of fear floating just below the surface of everyday life. It was felt most especially among members of the lower classes, who were largely defenseless against knights. Thus, a puzzling, frustrating, and ultimately terrible reality of medieval society, Kaeuper points out, was a seeming contradiction. "Chivalry could be praised to the heavens," he writes, "and at the same time it could be feared as a dark and sinister force."[38]

CHAPTER FOUR

Chivalry Flaunted: Tournaments and Heraldry

Medieval European knights were always concerned with their public image. In large part this was because their reputations as premiere fighters were central to their success in life, and they leaped at any chance either to maintain a good reputation or enhance one that did not seem good enough. It is not surprising, therefore, that knights frequently became involved in activities and endeavors that flaunted their abilities and chivalric ideals to the world.

The Knightly Orders

One avenue to this goal was to join an organization called an order. Each was a sort of brotherhood of knights who together dedicated themselves to some important task. Belonging to such an order brought a knight both honor and prestige, which significantly enhanced his reputation.

The first major knightly order was the Hospitallers, founded in 1113 during the early years of the crusading era. The initial members were merchants. They obtained permission from Muslim leaders then in control of the Holy Land to set up a hospital there for Christian pilgrims. Part of the deal was that the order be able to defend the hospital from would-be attackers. Hearing this, several wandering knights joined and offered their services. Over time more and more knights became Hospitallers, devoting themselves to protecting pilgrims, as well as providing care for soldiers wounded on the battlefield.

Of the several knightly orders that formed in the early High Middle Ages, the only other to rival the Hospitallers in size and fame was the Order of the Temple, better known as the Templar Knights. Established in about 1118 to 1120, the group dedicated itself to protecting the Temple Mount in Jerusalem, which the members believed was the site of King Solomon's temple in ancient times. Meanwhile, some Templars took a noncombatant role. They were bankers who collected donations made by wealthy Christians who desired to support crusaders fighting in the Holy Land.

One reason that the knights who joined these orders were seen as special was that, in military historian Philip Warner's words, "they were the bravest of the brave. They would fight to the death and never ask for surrender terms." In addition, he says, "their service to humanity should not be forgotten."[39] This was particularly true of the Hospitallers, who dealt with a feature of medieval warfare not often discussed—the fate of wounded soldiers. Arrows caused horribly painful wounds, and men crushed by heavy stones suffered unbelievable agony. Realizing this, Warner continues, the Hospitallers "introduced medical care to the battlefield and by skill and nursing restored to health many who would otherwise not have survived. When the scale of their resources is assessed, it is not surprising that these knights were widely renowned."[40]

Spectacle, Danger, and Hero Worship

Medieval knights also pursued more immediate and colorful venues in which to display themselves and their ideals to society. One was the tournament, a splendid combination of ceremony and public show sponsored by a king or other member of the nobility. In it knights clashed with one another in mock battles staged partly to entertain the spectators, but also to establish the fighters' reputations and abilities as warriors.

The Templar Knights were one of several knightly orders that formed in the High Middle Ages. Members of this order dedicated themselves to protecting the Temple Mount in Jerusalem. Artwork from the fourteenth century depicts Templar Knights standing watch in the Holy City.

These public displays involving knights were a big part of medieval pageantry. A major reason that such pageantry was highly effective was that it was eagerly sought after in an age in which organized, lively public entertainment was both uncommon and very expensive to stage. "Imagine a world where vivid color was a luxury," writes noted scholar Richard Barber. For centuries medieval Europe was a place

where entertainments might be seen at rare intervals, and then only in towns and cities; a world where after nightfall the darkness was broken by no more than a few feeble gleams. Today when our senses are bombarded with a surplus of riches, we can still respond to the pageantry of a great occasion. The effect on a medieval onlooker of such a pageant was many times more intense.[41]

Tournaments occupied the heart of much medieval pageantry, especially the entertainments staged by and mostly for the upper classes. They combined colorful spectacle with the thrills of a dangerous sport and the hero worship of star personalities. Medieval tournaments were also breeding grounds of romance. Young women came to see the chivalrous knights perform, not only to cheer them on but also to inspire them and in some cases to kindle an amorous relationship.

Practice for Real Combat

Exactly when and where the first tournaments were held is uncertain. But some evidence suggests it was in the late eleventh century (around 1070 to 1100) somewhere in northern France. The first versions were *mêlées*. Such an event was a staged battle fought across an area of several square miles of mostly open countryside.

During a typical mêlée, the knights made their way, either on horseback or on foot (or perhaps both in the course of a single event), through forests, vineyards, farmlands, and even villages. Sometimes they fought, and other times they maneuvered for advantage or waited in ambush. In some mêlées knights fought independently; in others they formed teams. In the larger tournaments each team could have upward of two hundred members.

WORDS IN CONTEXT

mêlée: A form of medieval tournament in which large numbers of knights fought one another across an area of several square miles.

The twelfth-century French writer Chretien de Troyes provided a description of a mêlée's opening moments, saying,

> The field is completely covered with [knights]. The ranks shudder on both sides, and from the clash there rises a loud din, with

a great cracking of lances. Lances break and shields are holed [pierced], the hauberks are torn and rent, saddles are emptied, and riders tumble, while the horses sweat and lather [foam at the mouth]. All draw their swords on those who clatter to the ground. Some rush up to accept their surrender, others in their defense.[42]

One of the primary motives for organizing such mock combats was to provide knights a chance to train in the use of various weapons and to rehearse battlefield tactics. "A mêlée tournament," Robert Jones explains, was

> an opportunity for the individual knight to practice and demonstrate his individual combat skills and for military households to learn to act together. And it reinforced their sense of cohesion and cooperation. It was also a place in which they could develop small-unit tactics in relative safety. Just as with other great knightly recreation, by ranging across the hill, fields, and through the woods of the tournament field the knight would learn much about the control of his horse and the use of terrain for advantage.[43]

Mêlées also gave knights a way to win money and valuables; the losers were expected to reward the winners with their own cash and possessions. This desire of many knights to enter tournaments mainly to fill their pockets is illustrated by a discussion between two medieval courtly ladies in a thirteenth-century document. Grinning, one lady tells the other, "It is not love that makes young knights brave. It is poverty!"[44]

The Coin of Success and Failure

In addition to these common reasons for entering tournaments, sometimes a knight did so because he had received a challenge from another knight. Apparently such a challenge could be issued in a number of

Trial by Combat

A particularly dangerous and brutal form of joust was a trial by combat, a form of *joûtes à outrance*. The two opponents agreed to settle a court case by fighting, and the victor on the field won the case. A famous example occurred in 1386 in France. A knight named Jean de Carouge was away on crusade, and another knight, Jacques de Gris, paid a visit to de Carouge's wife. She claimed that the visitor raped her. According to military historian Philip Warner, when de Carouge returned,

> he lost no time in applying to the king for permission to fight a duel to the death. The French king, Charles VI, was away at the time, but a *joûtes à outrance* was too good a spectacle to miss, and he hurried back to act as umpire. The first stage, on horseback, went off without injury to either, but when they dismounted to fight with swords, de Carouge sustained a serious wound in the thigh. In spite of this, he continued the battle and obtained his revenge with a sword thrust through de Gris's body. The latter died quickly but maintained his innocence of the accusation with his dying breath. Nevertheless, his body was given over to the common hangman and duly displayed on the gallows. Some years afterwards, another man made a deathbed confession to the crime. How the injured lady passed off this unfortunate discrepancy in her story is not recorded.

Philip Warner, *The Medieval Castle*. New York: Barnes and Noble, 1994, p. 99.

ways, including one described by the Byzantine princess Anna Comnena in her early twelfth-century historical account, the *Alexiad*. She quoted a French crusader knight she knew as saying, "At a crossroads in the country where I was born is an ancient shrine. To this, anyone

Jousting knights demonstrate their skills and treat spectators to a show filled with all the pageantry of a medieval tournament. Such spectacles combined both danger and sport.

who wishes to engage in single combat goes, prepared to fight. There he prays to God for help and there he stays awaiting the man who will dare to answer his challenge. At that crossroads I myself have spent time, waiting and longing for the man who would fight, but there was never one who dared."[45] If someone *had* accepted the French knight's challenge, the two men would have entered an upcoming tournament and fought each other in the mêlée.

To inform people of an upcoming tournament, the king, nobleman, or other sponsor sent heralds riding through the countryside to announce when and where it would be held. On the appointed day, historian Joseph Gies writes,

> the knights donned their armor, mounted their horses and lined up at opposite ends of a level meadow. At a flourish [trumpet signal] from a herald, the two bands of horsemen charged at each other. The field was open-ended because when one team was defeated and sought to retreat, the other, exactly as in real war, pursued it through woods and dale [valley] to capture prisoners. When it was all over, the defeated knights had to arrange with their captors for their ransom, usually the value of a horse and armor.[46]

Some knights made a regular living from collecting the valuables they won in tournaments. In a mere two years, for instance, the great English fighter William Marshal captured 103 knights during a series of mêlées. On the opposite side of this coin of success and failure, however, was the danger of serious injury or death. In addition to accidents, there were cases of treachery, in which someone purposely substituted a sharp sword for a blunted one, resulting in an opponent's death. There was also the risk of a knight losing his temper, killing one or more comrades, and expressing genuine sorrow afterward. In fact, few tournaments ended without either severe injury or death, or both, and on occasion the toll was especially grave. In 1241 in a mêlée at Neuss, in western Germany, some eighty knights were slaughtered.

Objections to the Violence

The deaths at Neuss were accidental. But every now and then a knight carrying a grudge issued a challenge to a personal enemy for a real fight, which became part of the tournament pageantry. Such events became known as *joûtes à outrance*, translating literally as "fights to the death."

Another form of violence that occurred from time to time at tournaments was fighting among the spectators. In 1250, for example, at Brackley in central England, a riot among the onlookers prompted King Henry III to issue a royal decree banning the tournament in the following year.

For a long time after tournaments first became common in Europe, the various forms of violence associated with them caused leading churchmen to express their disapproval. The clergy expected and accepted that people would die in wars. But they felt it was wrong for men, especially socially prominent ones like knights, to willingly risk their lives during peacetime for a mere sport. Hence some priests tried to discourage tournaments by threatening to deny the participants Christian burials. A decree issued in 1130 by the Council of Clermont, a clerical meeting attended by Pope Innocent II and many bishops, declared in part, "We condemn absolutely those detestable tournaments in which the knights usually come together by agreement and, to make a show of their strength and boldness, rashly engage in contests which are frequently the cause of death."[47]

No less troubling to churchmen was the fact that excessive amounts of eating, drinking, and sex were always part of the festivities at the tournaments. Hoping to reduce the incidence of such behavior, some bishops went so far as to threaten tournament contestants with excommunication—expulsion from the church. However, for close to two centuries knights across Europe generally ignored such threats, along with other efforts by church fathers to abolish the tournaments.

Nevertheless, objections to tournament violence by the clergy and others did have a modifying effect in the long run. By the early 1300s mêlées had become rare, and jousts had largely replaced them as the predominant kind of tournament. (The last mêlée on record took place in England in 1342.) A joust was a mock battle involving only two

The Rules of Heraldry

In this excerpt from his classic book on medieval chivalry, the late historian Maurice Keen explained that over time strict rules about the visual presentation of heraldry developed. (Keen uses an older spelling of *heraldic* in this excerpt.)

The arrangement and description of heraldric devices on a shield came to be regulated by well-defined rules (which in heraldric doctrine still hold). Thus the colors used in heraldry came to be limited to: *azur* (blue), *gules* (red), *vert* (green), *sable* (black), and *purpur* (purple); to the two metals, (gold), and *argent* (silver); and to the two furs, *ermine* and *vair*. The French of these technical terms is a sign of the predominant influence of French fashion in the early age of chivalry. There were soon more rules, too, as that which declares that color must not be laid upon color, nor metal upon metal. The ordinaries—the geometric patterns depicted on the shield, such as *chief* [bar running along the top edge], *fess* [bar running across the center], *chevron* [upside-down V shape], *bend* [bar running from the upper left corner to lower right corner, seen from the front], and *pale* [bar running vertically through the center]—came to be defined and limited in number. So also did the birds and beasts that were accepted as properly heraldric, and the objects commonly used in heraldry, such as *garbs* (sheaves of wheat), or the *manche* (the lady's sleeve with its overtones of courtly love).

Maurice Keen, *Chivalry*. New Haven, CT: Yale University Press, 2005, p. 129.

knights. The most common form consisted of the men charging at each other on horseback with couched lances, the object being to unseat one's opponent.

Vibrant Marks of Recognition

One important aspect of both mêlées and jousts was the spectators' ability to correctly identify the participants. This was difficult at first because these men wore extensive armor, including helmets that hid their facial features. "It was specially important," Maurice Keen explained, "to know who it was that one had unhorsed and might hope to take prisoner." Also, "a special significance was attached to the individual performance of particular knights in the field, whom judges and spectators must therefore be able to recognize. Hence, paintings on shields, which in the past had served merely decorative purpose, came to serve as marks of recognition."[48]

These colorful identifying insignia were heraldic devices, better known as coats of arms. They had existed for several centuries before the art form of heraldry began to emerge in the 1100s but had been used primarily as decorations. With the rise of chivalry, however, in which knights found it important to flaunt their martial skills and deeds, it became essential to recognize instantly specific fighters.

In his twelfth-century work *Lancelot, or the Knight of the Cart*, Chretien de Troyes penned a passage that gives a vivid description of the use of heraldry by knights in conflict. In it a knight who is sitting out a major tournament gives a queen standing beside him a running commentary: "Do you see that knight yonder with a golden band across his red shield? [He is] Governauz of Roberdic. And do you see that other one, who has an eagle and a dragon painted side by side on his shield? That is the son of the king of Aragon, who has come to this land in search of glory and renown."[49]

At first displayed primarily on knights' shields, heraldic devices came to decorate their surcoats, banners attached to their horses, and

58

even their tomb markers. Moreover, individual knights were not the only ones identified. Coats of arms also denoted the noble families they belonged to, making them enthusiastic expressions of one's pride of birth. Medieval knights and the often bloody contests they engaged in disappeared at the close of the Middle Ages. But much of the heraldry they had proudly displayed survived across Europe and beyond, an eternal and visually stunning memory of the vibrant pageantry of a remarkable bygone age.

CHAPTER FIVE

Knights' Demise and Their Legacy

For close to five hundred years, knights had dominated European warfare and held an esteemed position in medieval society. Yet as Robert Jones points out, "By 1600 that dominance had gone." The image of the knight as a fighter widely seen as superior to and feared by all others "had vanished from the battlefield."[50]

Knights still served in European armies. But they could no longer be distinguished from what the English called the gentry. These were middle-class and upper-class men with no knightly training or status. Nevertheless, they served, as Frances Gies says, as "men-at-arms who wore the same armor, rode the same horses, and came to earn the same pay."[51] This merging of knights into a sort of generic cavalry was a definite step down in status and prestige for the knights of old.

At the same time, the knight's social role blended with that of members of the gentry, who steadily distinguished themselves more in government administration than in military service. Serving as aides to kings, aristocrats, and political leaders came to have equal dignity to fighting on the battlefield. The rising complexity of local and national governments, Jones explains, meant that duties earlier performed mainly by knights "were opened up to those of lesser social rank. Men of gentry rank, who once would have been considered too lacking in honor for the role and, a generation or so earlier would have been donning the harness of a man-at-arms, now put on the robes of the political aide and lawyer and in doing so acquired noble status."[52]

Three Major Military Changes

The specific changes that altered and lessened the key military role of knights fell into three main categories—economic, strategic, and technological. First, economic factors steadily made knights too specialized and expensive for national armies to maintain. In part this was because their extensive armor became incredibly pricey, making it unrealistic to field large numbers of these special warriors. Also, such fighters were useful mainly in large-scale charges in big pitched battles. But those events were increasingly rare—another reason that knights were no longer cost-effective.

The strategic changes that steadily marginalized knights during the sixteenth century involved the increasing importance of infantry on the battlefield. More and more, military commanders used huge blocks of foot soldiers, each up to four thousand strong. Some were armed with advanced crossbows, and others created forest-like masses of long, outstretched pikes. Even a line of charging knights, once the ultimate shock force in warfare, could do little to dent such a formidable barrier.

The technological change that helped doom the traditional knight in battle was the arming of increasing numbers of infantrymen with a completely new and devastating weapon. By the late 1500s handheld guns had come into wide use in warfare. Not only did the loud noises and smoke they produced frighten knights' horses, but the bullets fired by the guns penetrated all but the heaviest plate armor. Making armor even thicker and heavier proved impractical. So over time commanders ordered their cavalry to abandon most armor, along with the lance, and to arm themselves with smaller versions of the guns used by foot soldiers. In these ways the heavily armored knight quickly disappeared from the battlefield.

Ridiculing the Knights of Old

The steady demise of traditional knights saw the corresponding loss of their personal, distinctive, and in many ways purely ideal code of

A wheel lock pistol, dating from 1578 and made from steel, walnut, and staghorn, is but one example of the handheld guns that came into wide use in the 1500s. The appearance of guns on the battlefield signaled the approaching end to the era of the knights.

behavior. Without a strong knightly class to promote chivalry, its ideals increasingly came to be seen as old-fashioned. Similarly, the supposedly superior military man who swore gallant oaths and constantly strove for perfection became more than outdated. The image of the old-style chivalric knight became a sort of cartoon, a pathetic portrayal of a hopeless fool who should be ignored or ridiculed.

Spanish novelist Miguel de Cervantes (1547–1616) captured this sad sentiment better than anyone else of his time. He lived in the same era in which the conventional knight was disappearing from Europe, and the fact that he wrote about something he witnessed firsthand gave his 1605 novel *Don Quixote* a special power and impact. "His brain addled by reading too much chivalric literature," Gies recounts, the aged Quixote "rides through the countryside on his worn out horse, in rusty armor and pasteboard helmet, fighting mule drivers, windmills, and flocks of sheep in the name of his 'lady,' in reality nothing more than a good-looking country wench. After a long succession of disillusioning experiences, he rejects on his death-bed 'all profane stories of knight-errantry.'"[53]

Having the fictional would-be knight Quixote give up reading the chivalric romances served Cervantes's purpose of poking fun at the knights of old. In the real world, however, those romances became one of the most enduring legacies that medieval knights gave to later generations. The hefty body of surviving chivalric literature celebrates the heroism of various knights, some of them real, others fictional. It also rejoices in their sense of honor and in some cases their deep Christian faith.

Tales of Legendary Founders

The most famous characters from the British portion of this knightly literature are King Arthur and his heroic knights of the Round Table—among them Sir Lancelot and Sir Galahad. Many dozens of myths and stories about their bravery and noble deeds have survived. Together, they form the Arthurian collection of myths, which is read worldwide and studied in college courses. Also, many modern residents of England and Wales look back on Arthur with pride. They view his legendary kingdom of Camelot, a land literally built on the ideals of knightly chivalry, as the first ancient germ of what would eventually become the modern nation of Britain.

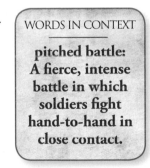

WORDS IN CONTEXT

pitched battle: A fierce, intense battle in which soldiers fight hand-to-hand in close contact.

In the French portion of the surviving heroic literature about knights, the most renowned characters are the Frankish emperor Charlemagne and his military officer Roland. *The Song of Roland*, whose author remains unknown, dates to sometime between 1140 and 1170. The story takes place much earlier, in the 770s, and deals with Charlemagne's and Roland's betrayal by another French knight.

That treachery leads to a savage battle. Roland and the knights he commands are ambushed by an army of Arabs, and despite his moving display of heroism, Roland dies. Later, Charlemagne utterly defeats the intruders, thereby achieving revenge for Roland's death. Because the early modern French viewed Charlemagne as the creator of the French nation, *The Song of Roland* became and remains France's national epic. Thus, for the British, French, and others who love traditional European literature, medieval knights and chivalry live on in the romantic tales of those legendary founders of nations.

Novels and Films About Knights

Moreover, such antiquated texts are not the only form of literature that keeps the world of knights and chivalry alive and fresh. A stream of modern novels about knights and their exploits began with Cervantes's *Don Quixote* in the early seventeenth century and has not let up since.

WORDS IN CONTEXT

knight-errantry:
In romantic
medieval
literature, the
practice of a
knight traveling
in search of
wrongs to right.

Among the other great classics of the genre are Sir Walter Scott's *Ivanhoe* (1819), the exciting tale of a knight who returns to England from the Crusades and joins forces with Robin Hood to oppose a cast of villains; Mark Twain's *A Connecticut Yankee in King Arthur's Court* (1889), a skillful blend of Arthurian romance, time travel, and witty humor; and Howard Pyle's *Men of Iron* (1891), a vivid story of a young squire who trains hard to become a knight so he can restore his father's tarnished reputation.

The twentieth and early twenty-first centuries have had their own share of worthy novels about knighthood. Particularly noteworthy is T.H. White's tale of the young King Arthur, *The Once and Future King* (1958), which inspired the classic Broadway musical *Camelot* (1960). Other worthwhile examples include Samuel Shellabarger's *Prince of Foxes* (1947); Robyn Young's *The Fall of the Templars* (2010); and Bernard Cornwell's *1356* (2013).

Camelot was not the only successful Broadway show about knights and chivalry. In 1965 New York audiences thrilled to the opening of *Man of La Mancha*, a spectacular musical based on Cervantes's *Don Quixote*. Richard Kiley won a Tony Award for his portrayal of both Quixote and Cervantes, whose onstage character narrates the wannabe knight's story.

A Romantic Blaze of Glory

Today, just as King Arthur and his knights embody the chivalric spirit of early Britain, the Frankish emperor Charlemagne and his trusty knight Roland symbolize the noble spirit of France's founding heroes. In *The Song of Roland*, the oldest surviving major work of French literature, Roland's stepfather turns traitor and aids an army of Arabs from Spain. They ambush a force of Franks led by Roland and his friend, the bold knight Oliver, at Roncevals in northern Spain. The narrative of the battle is detailed and filled with descriptions of superhuman feats of swordplay by the Frankish knights. In a startling display of chivalric bravery, for instance, Oliver draws his sword and attacks an enemy officer. "He severs his head in twain," the text reads, "cuts through his embroidered [chest protector] and his body, through his good saddle set with gold, and severs the backbone of his steed, and that man and horse fall dead on the field before him. Then said Roland, 'Now I hold you as my brother, and 'tis for such feats the emperor loves us!'"

A different aspect of chivalry is depicted later in the battle, when the stricken Roland is about to die. He confesses his sins and in a pious gesture holds his glove up to God. These acts are rewarded as Gabriel and other angels suddenly appear, embrace the knight as he dies, and in a romantic blaze of glory carry his soul away to heaven.

Isabel Butler, ed., *The Song of Roland*, in *Modern Literature in Translation*, translated by C.W. Jones. New York: Longmans, Green, 1950, pp. 553–54.

Man of La Mancha became a movie in 1972, with English actor Peter O'Toole in the dual lead role. Not long before, in 1967, a colorful film version of the musical *Camelot* had appeared, starring Richard Harris as King Arthur.

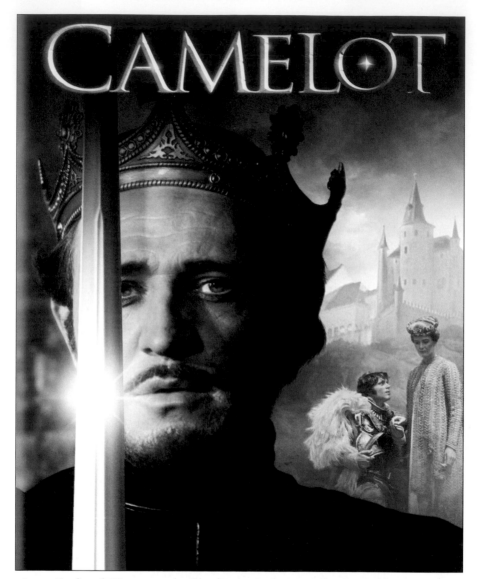

Actor Richard Harris starred as King Arthur in the 1967 film Camelot, *an idealized version of the myths of King Arthur and his heroic knights of the Round Table. Other films and many books have depicted the Arthurian legends in a variety of ways.*

These two filmed musicals are among numerous movies depicting knights and their adventures. One of the best is Russian director Sergei Eisenstein's *Alexander Nevsky* (1938), about the defeat of the fearsome Teutonic knights by medieval Russian hero Nevsky; the film's shattering clash of thousands of knights on a frozen lake is one of the greatest battle scenes ever filmed. Other first-rate movies about knighthood are Anthony Mann's *El Cid* (1961), the story of the famous noble Spanish knight of that name; Franklin Shaffner's *The War Lord* (1965), with highly realistic scenes of knights waging siege warfare; and John Boorman's *Excalibur* (1981), a visually beautiful telling of several of the Arthurian romances.

Reproducing the Knight's World

The motion picture is not the only modern visual art form, institution, or other venue that has embraced the memory and colorful imagery of the medieval European knight. Others include graphic novels, video and role-playing games, museums, sculptures in churches, and numerous others. Yet arguably the most popular element of the medieval knight's modern legacy consists of the hundreds of full-scale, live reenactments held around the globe each year. Several attract players, appropriately called reenactors, and spectators that together number in the hundreds of thousands.

Many of these stylish events have come to be known as medieval or Renaissance fairs or festivals. They seek to reproduce the overall atmosphere of Europe in the High Middle Ages, and knights are always among the most important and popular characters depicted. Most medieval festivals attempt to maintain historical accuracy. To that end, the participants dress in appropriate costumes and wield tools, weapons, and other props that fit the specific medieval period depicted.

Some of the reenactors in the festivals entertain spectators by performing authentic music of that age, while others make and sell medieval-style crafts and foods. Meanwhile, for many fairgoers the major highlight is when men dressed as knights present exciting staged sword fights and jousts. One of the biggest and most popular events of this type in the United States is the Bristol Renaissance Fair in Bristol, Wisconsin. Set in England in the 1500s, it draws up to two hundred thousand fairgoers annually.

Modern Games Featuring Knights

The electronic video game is among the many modern media and entertainment venues that have come to feature medieval knights. One of the more popular examples is *Age of Chivalry*, released in 2007. As in a majority of such games, the players must try to achieve an objective, in this case gaining control of a fictional medieval kingdom. Two teams of players representing knights—the "good" Agatha Knights and the "evil" Mason Order—seek to achieve that control by engaging in battles and sieges. Other popular video games of the genre include *Knights of Honor* (2005), *Chivalry: Medieval Warfare* (2012), and *Stronghold Kingdoms* (2012).

Some modern knights and chivalry enthusiasts prefer the more traditional role-playing game, often called the RPG for short. (Both electronic and nonelectronic versions exist.) In contests that can go on for weeks or even months, the players take on the personas of knights and other characters who develop and interact over time, eventually reaching some sort of goal. A well-known example, *Stronghold Crusader* (2008), is set during the Crusades and deals with real historical battles and events, including the siege of Jerusalem by Christian knights in the First Crusade. Another popular example, *Knights of the Nile* (2006), introduces various elements of fantasy. The players must obtain the aid of the spirits of some deceased knights in order to foil an evil king.

Even more trendy in recent years is the growing phenomenon of full-scale reenactments of medieval combat, in which knights are the biggest attraction. Some of these enormous spectacles restage actual historical battles, when possible on the same sites where they originally took place. For the sake of safety, the participants most often use blunted weapons.

These events are especially popular in Britain, where more than three thousand avid reenactors converge annually to bring to life the pivotal 1066 Battle of Hastings. Other important British battles reenacted are the ones at Bosworth Field (1485), in which the famous monarch Richard III met his end; and Bannockburn (1314), which paved the way for Scottish independence from England. In such mock battles, the participants try to reproduce faithfully what actually happened in the real versions.

Knights All Around Us

The biggest medieval combat reenactment group in the world is the Society for Creative Anachronism, or SCA, established in 1966. (An anachronism is something seen or used today that belongs to a prior century or era.) Local chapters, each called a "kingdom," exist across the United States, Canada, Australia, New Zealand, Europe, South Africa, Panama, South Korea, and elsewhere. In 2013 the combined kingdoms had some thirty thousand nearly full-time members and another thirty thousand part-time helpers and other associates.

Wearing full and authentic-looking armor, the SCA reenactors bring to life swordplay, jousts, and other combat by medieval knights. The leading victor of a local series of bouts becomes ruler of the kingdom for a year. These latter-day knights are not like the warriors in Renaissance fairs, "where the fighting is staged," journalist Kyle Swenson reports. By contrast, he says, the SCA action is "hard-core," and "brute force determines who will be king. Each fighter has to be outfitted with a set of historically accurate armor, including neck, torso, knee, and elbow protection made out of metal or heavy leather. Each helmet must be made of steel . . . [and some participants] spend up to $5,000 on suits made by master blacksmiths."[54]

The continual growth of modern medieval reenactments, along with the widespread popularity of knights in all kinds of literature and media, attest to a striking reality. In spectacular fashion, the imposing image of the medieval European knight outlived the era that both created him and

Wearing authentic-looking clothing and armor, reenactors take part in one of the many medieval festivals that take place today around the world. Some of these festivals feature staged fighting and other events that were common during medieval times.

held him and his code of honor in awe. Indeed, today European knights remain instantly recognizable and exceptionally captivating. As Robert Jones puts it, "All around us, in the arms and armor displayed in museums, in the funeral monuments and coats of arms in countless churches and cathedrals, in the manuscript illuminations [decorations] and the stories and tales of great battles and heroic deeds, the color and pageantry of the world of the warrior still exerts its fascination."[55]

SOURCE NOTES

Introduction: An Ongoing Fascination for Knights

1. John the Troubadour, *History of William Marshal*, vol. 2, ed. A.J. Holden, trans. S. Gregory and D. Crouch. London: Anglo-Norman Text Society, 2004, p. 51.
2. Robert Jones, *Knight: The Warrior and World of Chivalry*. Oxford, UK: Osprey, 2011, p. 11.
3. Jones, *Knight*, p. 8.
4. Oskar H. Sommer, ed., *The Vulgate Version of the Arthurian Romances, Edited from Manuscripts in the British Museum*, vol. 3. New York: AMS, 1969, pp. 113–14.

Chapter One: The Rise of the Medieval Knight

5. Jones, *Knight*, p. 20.
6. Arther Ferrill, *The Fall of the Roman Empire: The Military Explanation*. New York: Thames and Hudson, 1986, p. 84.
7. Ferrill, *The Fall of the Roman Empire*, p. 85.
8. C. Warren Hollister, *Medieval Europe: A Short History*. New York: McGraw-Hill, 1998, p. 100.
9. David Nicolle, *The Age of Charlemagne*. Oxford, UK: Osprey, 1999, p. 7.
10. Quoted in A.J. Grant, ed. and trans., *Early Lives of Charlemagne by Eginhard the Monk of St. Gall*. London: Chatto & Windus, 1926, pp. 145–46.
11. Nicolle, *The Age of Charlemagne*, p. 7.
12. Nicolle, *The Age of Charlemagne*, p. 14.
13. Bernard S. Bachrach, "Early Medieval Europe," in *War and Society in the Ancient and Medieval Worlds*: Asia, *The Mediterranea, Europe, and Mesoamerica*, ed. Kurt Raaflaub and Nathan Rosenstein. Cambridge, MA: Harvard University Press, 1999, p. 292.

Chapter Two: The Height of Knights in War and Society

14. Frances Gies, *The Knight in History*. New York: Harper Collins, 2011, p. 4.

15. Gies, *The Knight in History*, p. 4.
16. Archer Jones, *The Art of War in the Western World*. New York: Oxford University Press, 2001, pp. 151–52.
17. Jones, *Knight*, p. 45.
18. James F. Dunnigan and Albert A. Nofi, "Medieval Warfare," *Hundred Years War*. www.hyw.com.
19. Marc Bloch, *Feudal Society*, vol. 2. London: Routledge, 1989, p. 295.
20. Frances Gies and Joseph Gies, *Life in a Medieval Castle*. New York: Harper & Row, 1979, p. 174.
21. Quoted in Leon Gautier, *Chivalry*, trans. Henry Frith. Whitefish, MT: Kessinger, 2007, p. 123.
22. Quoted in Marjorie Rowling, *Everyday Life in Medieval Times*. New York: Dorset, 1987, p. 40.

Chapter Three: Code of Chivalry: Ideal Versus Reality

23. Maurice Keen, *Chivalry*. New Haven, CT: Yale University Press, 2005, p. 252.
24. Jones, *Knight*, p. 144.
25. Quoted in Linda Paterson, "Knights and the Concept of Knighthood in the Twelfth-Century Occitan Epic," in *Forum for Modern Language Studies*, vol. 17, 1981, pp. 116, 120–21, 128.
26. Quoted in Keen, *Chivalry*, p. 80.
27. Richard W. Kaeuper, *Chivalry and Violence in Medieval Europe*. New York: Oxford University Press, 2001, p. 48.
28. Quoted in Carl Erdmann, *The Origins of the Idea of Crusade*. Princeton, NJ: Princeton University Press, 1977, pp. 336–37.
29. Quoted in Conrad Greenia, trans., *The Works of Bernard of Clairvaux*, vol. 7. Kalamazoo, MI: Cistercian Fathers, 1977, p. 129.
30. Quoted in Bloch, *Feudal Society*, vol. 2, p. 293.
31. Roger of Wendover, *Flowers of History*, vol. 2, ed. J. A. Giles. London: Bohn, 1849, pp. 396–97.
32. Quoted in Bloch, *Feudal Society*, vol. 2, p. 293.
33. Kaeuper, *Chivalry and Violence in Medieval Europe*, p. 29.
34. Quoted in William W. Kibbler, ed. and trans., *Lancelot, Part V*. New London: CT, Garland, 1995, p. 197.

35. Quoted in Geoffrey Brereton, ed. and trans., *Froissart's Chronicles,* 3rd ed. Baltimore, MD: Penguin, 1968, pp. 222–24.

36. Kaeuper, *Chivalry and Violence in Medieval Europe*, p. 95.

37. Kaeuper, *Chivalry and Violence in Medieval Europe*, p. 95.

38. Kaeuper, *Chivalry and Violence in Medieval Europe*, p. 29.

Chapter Four: Chivalry Flaunted: Tournaments and Heraldry

39. Philip Warner, *The Medieval Castle*. New York: Barnes and Noble, 1994, p. 129.

40. Warner, *The Medieval Castle*, p. 129.

41. Richard Barber and Juliet Barker, *Tournaments*. Woodbridge, UK: Boydell, 2013, p. 1.

42. Chretien de Troyes, *Eric et Enid*, in *Four Arthurian Romances*, trans. D.D.R. Owen. London: Dent, 1987, p. 28.

43. Jones, *Knight*, p. 88.

44. Quoted in Keen, *Chivalry*, p. 88.

45. Anna Comnena, *Alexiad*, ed. and trans. E.R.A. Sewter. Harmondsworth, UK: Penguin, 1979, p. 326.

46. Gies and Gies, *Life in a Medieval Castle*, p. 178.

47. Quoted in *Medieval Sourcebook*, "Tenth Ecumenical Council," Fordham University, November 1996. www.fordham.edu.

48. Keen, *Chivalry*, p. 125.

49. Chretien de Troyes, *Lancelot, or The Knight of the Cart* in *Four Arthurian Romances*. eBooks@Adelaide. http://ebooks.adelaide.edu.au.

Chapter Five: Knights' Demise and Their Legacy

50. Jones, *Knight*, p. 212.

51. Gies, *The Knight in History*, p. 197.

52. Jones, *Knight*, p. 214.

53. Gies, *The Knight in History*, p. 204.

54. Kyle Swenson, "Weekend Warriors of A.D. 450," *Week*, August 30, 2013, p. 36.

55. Jones, *Knight*, p. 223.

FOR FURTHER RESEARCH

Books

Charles Addison, *The History of the Knights Templar*. Oxford, UK: Acheron, 2012.

Toney Allman, *Life in Medieval Times*. San Diego: Reference-Point, 2014.

Richard Barber and Juliet Barker, *Tournaments*. Woodbridge, UK: Boydell, 2013.

Jane Bingham, *Internet-Linked Medieval World*. London: Usborne, 2012.

David Crouch, *William Marshal: Knighthood, War, and Chivalry, 1147–1219*. New York: Pearson, 2010.

Stephen Currie, *The Medieval Castle*. San Diego: ReferencePoint, 2013.

Frances Gies, *The Knight in History*. New York: HarperCollins, 2011.

Robert Jones, *Knight: The Warrior and World of Chivalry*. Oxford, UK: Osprey, 2011.

Richard W. Kaeuper, *Chivalry and Violence in Medieval Europe*. New York: Oxford University Press, 2001.

Maurice Keen, *Chivalry*. New Haven, CT: Yale University Press, 2005.

Andrew Langley, *Medieval Life*. New York: Dorling Kindersley, 2011.

David Nicolle, *European Medieval Tactics, 1260–1500*. Oxford, UK: Osprey, 2012.

Charles Phillips, *The Illustrated History of Knights and Crusades: A Visual Account of the Medieval Knight*. London: Anness, 2011.

Bernard Quaritch, *A Catalogue of Medieval Literature, Especially the Romances of Chivalry*. Charleston, SC: Nabu, 2010.

Nigel Saul, *Chivalry in Medieval England*. Cambridge, MA: Harvard University Press, 2011.

Jeffrey L. Singman, *The Middle Ages: Everyday Life in Medieval Europe*. New York: Sterling, 2013.

Internet Sources

Richard Abels, "Medieval Chivalry," US Naval Academy. www.usna.edu /Users/history/abels/hh381/Chivalry.htm.

James McDonald, "William Marshal: The Flower of Chivalry," Medieval Warfare. www.medievalwarfare.info/marshal.htm.

Medieval-Life.net, "Training a Knight," 2000. www.medieval-life.net /knight_training.htm.

Albert A. Nofi and James F. Dunnigan, "Chivalry," *Hundred Years' War*. www.hyw.com/books/history/Chivalry.htm.

James G. Patterson, "The Myth of the Mounted Knight," ORB: Online Reference Book for Medieval Studies. www.the-orb.net/non_spec /missteps/ch3.html.

Websites

Crusades (www.medieval-life-and-times.info/crusades). An easy-to-read general synopsis of the Crusades, with several links to sites about the various knights who fought in these wars.

Medieval History in the Movies, Fordham University (www.fordham .edu/Halsall/medfilms.asp#feudalism). This spirited and worthwhile overview of films set in the Middle Ages includes a section on movies featuring knights.

Medieval Warfare (www.hyw.com/books/history/Medi0000.htm). Part of a useful online overview of medieval times, this is an enlightening collection of facts about war and weapons in that pivotal period.

Medieval Weapons & Armor (www.medievalwarfare.info/weapons.htm). A visually beautiful presentation of the various kinds of armor and weapons used by medieval European knights, with excellent written descriptions of each.

Selected Sources: France, *Internet Medieval Sourcebook* (www.ford ham.edu/Halsall/sbook1m.asp). A collection of primary source writings from early medieval France, the place and period in which Frankish warriors laid the groundwork for the knightly class to come.

INDEX

PICTURE CREDITS

Cover: Investiture of a Knight, from the 'Metz Codex', 1290 (vellum), French School, (13th century)/Private Collection/Index/The Bridgeman Art Library

Mary Aaseng: 9

© Corbis: 43

Photofest Pictures: 66

Thinkstock Images: 4, 5, 70

The Entrance of Alexander the Great (356–23 BC) into Babylon (oil on canvas), Diziani, Gasparo (1689–1767)/Musee des Beaux-Arts, Dijon, France/Giraudon/The Bridgeman Art Library: 13

Emperor Charlemagne (747–814) and his Army fighting the Saracens in Spain, 778 from the Story of Ogier (vellum), Verard, Antoine (1450-1519)/ Private Collection/Roger-Viollet, Paris/The Bridgeman Art Library: 17

Leather jerkin, c.1560 (leather), English School, (16th century)/© Museum of London, UK/The Bridgeman Art Library: 22

Gothic armour for man and horse (metal), German School, (15th century)/ Royal Armouries, Leeds, UK/The Bridgeman Art Library: 27

Ms Fr 6465 f.25 Death of Clothar I (d.561) and the division of his kingdom, Grandes Chroniques de France (vellum), Fouquet, Jean (c.1420–80)/Bibliotheque Nationale, Paris, France/The Bridgeman Art Library: 31

The Arming and Departure of the Knights, tapestry designed by the artist and woven by Morris & Co., 1895–96 (textile), Burne-Jones, Sir Edward Coley (1833–98)/Birmingham Museums and Art Gallery/The Bridgeman Art Library: 39

Knights Templar before Jerusalem, from Le Roman de Godefroi de Bouillon (vellum), French School, (14th century)/Bibliotheque Nationale, Paris, France/The Bridgeman Art Library: 50

Richard III (1452–85) from 'Above and Below Stairs', Goodall, John Strickland (1908–96)/Private Collection/© Christopher Wood Gallery, London, UK/The Bridgeman Art Library: 54

Wheel-lock hunting pistol, 1578 (steel, walnut & stag horn), German School, (16th century)/Cleveland Museum of Art, OH, USA/Gift of Mr. and Mrs. John L. Severance/The Bridgeman Art Library: 62